Medium - Advanced

FANFARE AND FLOURISHES

for a Festive Occasion

for Brass Quintet and Organ

James Curnow

CURNOW®
MUSIC

EXCLUSIVELY DISTRIBUTED BY

HAL•LEONARD®
CORPORATION

7777 W. BLUEMOUND RD. P.O. BOX 13819 MILWAUKEE, WI 53213

Edition Number: CMP 1051-05

Fanfare and Flourishes
for a Festive Occasion
for Brass Quintet and Organ
James Curnow

ISBN 90-431-2386-2

© **Copyright 2005 by Curnow Music Press, Inc.**

P.O. Box 142, Wilmore KY 40390, USA

James Curnow

James Curnow was born in Port Huron, Michigan and raised in Royal Oak, Michigan. He lives in Nicholasville, Kentucky where he is president, composer, and educational consultant for Curnow Music Press, Inc. of Lexington, Kentucky, publishers of significant music for concert band and brass band. He also serves as Composer-in-residence (Emeritus) on the faculty of Asbury College in Wilmore, Kentucky, and is editor of all music publications for The Salvation Army in Atlanta, Georgia.

His formal training was received at Wayne State University (Detroit, Michigan) and at Michigan State University (East Lansing, Michigan), where he was a euphonium student of Leonard alcone, and a conducting student of Dr. Harry Begian. His studies in composition and arranging were with F. Maxwell Wood, James Gibb, Jere Hutchinson, and Irwin Fischer.

James Curnow has taught in all areas of instrumental music, both in the public schools (five years), and on the college and university level (twenty-six years). He is a member of several professional organizations, including the American Bandmasters Association, College Band Directors National Association, World Association of Symphonic Bands and Wind Ensembles and the American Society of Composers, Authors and Publishers (ASCAP). In 1980 he received the National Band Association's Citation of Excellence. In 1985, while a tenured Associate Professor at the University of Illinois, Champaign-Urbana, Mr. Curnow was honored as an outstanding faculty member. Among his most recent honors are inclusion in Who's Who in America, Who's Who in the South and Southwest, and Composer of the Year (1997) by the Kentucky Music Teachers Association and the National Music Teachers Association. He has received annual ASCAP standard awards since 1979.

As a conductor, composer and clinician, Curnow has traveled throughout the United States, Canada, Australia, Japan and Europe where his music has received wide acclaim. He has won several awards for band compositions including the ASBDA/Volkwein Composition Award in 1977 (Symphonic Triptych) and 1979 (Collage for Band), the ABA/Ostwald Award in 1980 (Mutanza) and 1984 (Symphonic Variants for Euphonium and Band), the 1985 Sixth International Competition of Original Compositions for Band (Australian Variants Suite), and the 1994 Coup de Vents Composition Competition of Le Havre, France (Lochinvar).

Curnow has been commissioned to write over two hundred works for concert band, brass band, orchestra, choir and various vocal and instrumental ensembles. His published works now number well over four hundred. His most recent commissions include the Tokyo Symphony Orchestra (Symphonic Variants for Euphonium and Orchestra), the United States Army Band (Pershing's Own, Washington, D.C.-Lochinvar, Symphonic Poem for Winds and Percussion), Roger Behrend and the DEG Music Products, Inc. and Willson Band Instrument Companies (Concerto for Euphonium and Orchestra), the Olympic Fanfare and Theme for the Olympic Flag (Atlanta Committee for the Olympic Games, 1996), the Kentucky Music Teachers Association/National Music Teachers Association in 1997 (On Poems of John Keats for String Quartet) and Michigan State University Bands (John Whitwell, Director of Bands) in honor of David Catron's twenty-six years of service to the university and the university bands (Ode And Epinicion).

FANFARE AND FLOURISHES
for a Festive Occasion
for Brass Quintet and Organ

James Curnow

Program Note

Based on Marc-Antoine Charpentier's (1634-1704) "Te Deum", Fanfare and Flourishes for a Festive Occasion was commissioned for the 1991 European Brass Band Championships held in Rotterdam, Holland. The premiere performance was given by the Black Dyke Mills Brass Band during the Gala Concert. The symphonic band version was commissioned by the Alfred M. Barbe High School Symphonic Band, Lake Charles, Louisiana, Steve Hand, Conductor.

Note to the Contuctor

As with any fanfare, this one must be approached with flare and energy while maintaining an exacting tempo and marcato style. Close attention will need to be given to the triplet figures in the brasses, emphasizing an even tempo and length for all eighth notes. It is also important to avoid the natural tendencies both to rush the faster passages and to let the dynamics dictate tempo.

Instrumentation:

Conductor
Bb Trumpet 1
Bb Trumpet 2
F Horn
Trombone
Tuba
Eb Bass T.C.
Organ

FANFARE AND FLOURISHES
For A Festive Occasion
(For Brass Quintet and Organ)

James Curnow (ASCAP)

Copyright © 2005 by Curnow Music Press, Inc.
P.O. Box 142, Wilmore, KY 40390, USA
Edition Number: CMP 1051-05

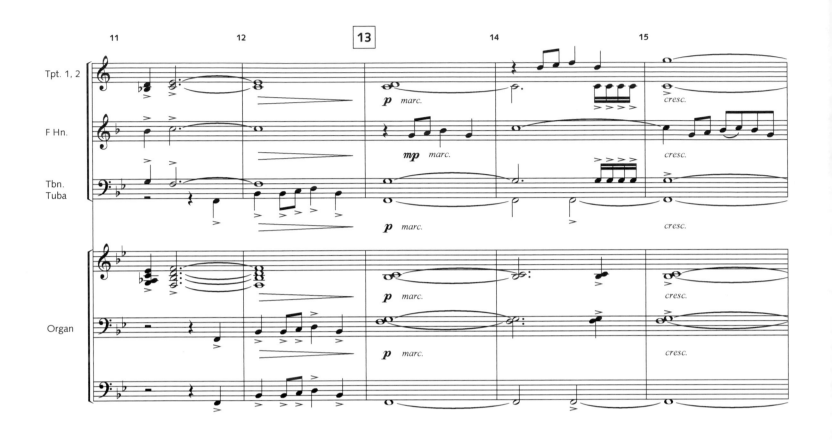

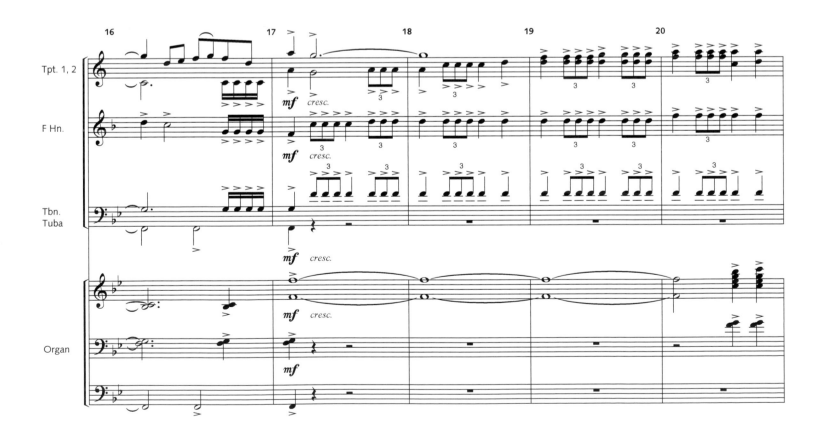

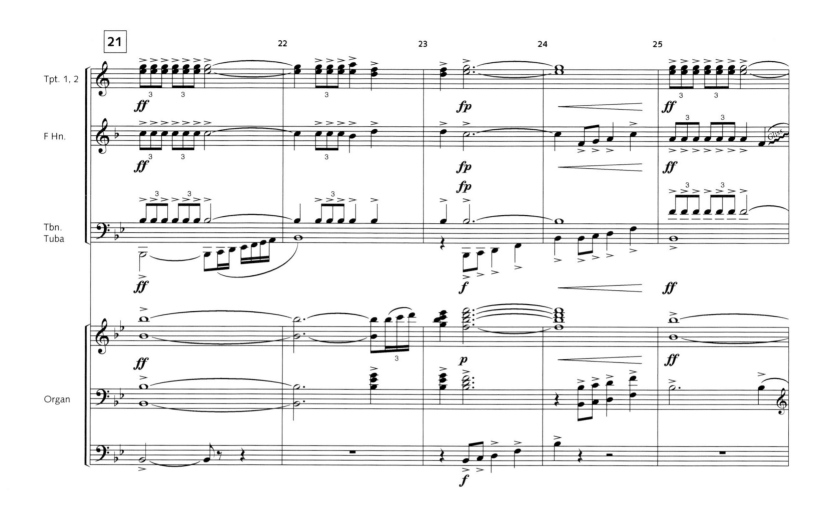

FANFARE AND FLOURISHES
For A Festive Occasion
(For Brass Quintet and Organ)

Bb TRUMPET 1

James Curnow (ASCAP)

Copyright © 2005 by Curnow Music Press, Inc.
P.O. Box 142, Wilmore, KY 40390, USA
Edition Number: CMP 1051-05

FANFARE AND FLOURISHES

Bb TRUMPET 2

James Curnow (ASCAP)

For A Festive Occasion
(For Brass Quintet and Organ)

Copyright © 2005 by **Curnow Music Press, Inc.**
P.O. Box 142, Wilmore, KY 40390, USA
Edition Number: CMP 1051-05

F HORN

FANFARE AND FLOURISHES

James Curnow (ASCAP)

For A Festive Occasion
(For Brass Quintet and Organ)

Copyright © 2005 by Curnow Music Press, Inc.
P.O. Box 142, Wilmore, KY 40390, USA
Edition Number: CMP 1051-05

TROMBONE

FANFARE AND FLOURISHES

James Curnow (ASCAP)

For A Festive Occasion
(For Brass Quintet and Organ)

Copyright © 2005 by Curnow Music Press, Inc.
P.O. Box 142, Wilmore, KY 40390, USA
Edition Number: CMP 1051-05

FANFARE AND FLOURISHES

Tuba

James Curnow (ASCAP)

For A Festive Occasion
(For Brass Quintet and Organ)

Copyright © 2005 by Curnow Music Press, Inc.
P.O. Box 142, Wilmore, KY 40390, USA
Edition Number: CMP 1051-05

Eb BASS

FANFARE AND FLOURISHES

James Curnow (ASCAP)

For A Festive Occasion
(For Brass Quintet and Organ)

Copyright © 2005 by Curnow Music Press, Inc.
P.O. Box 142, Wilmore, KY 40390, USA
Edition Number: CMP 1051-05

FANFARE AND FLOURISHES

James Curnow (ASCAP)

For A Festive Occasion

(For Brass Quintet and Organ)

Copyright © 2005 by **Curnow Music Press, Inc.**
P.O. Box 142, Wilmore, KY 40390, USA
Edition Number: CMP 1051-05

48

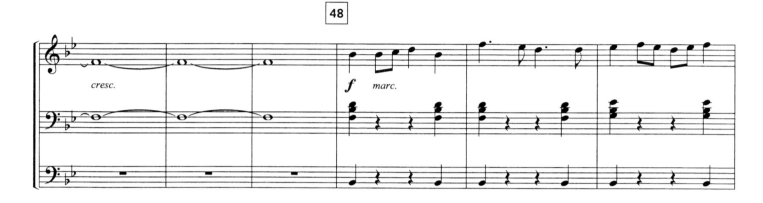

56

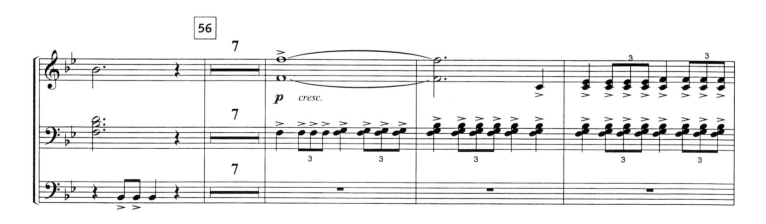

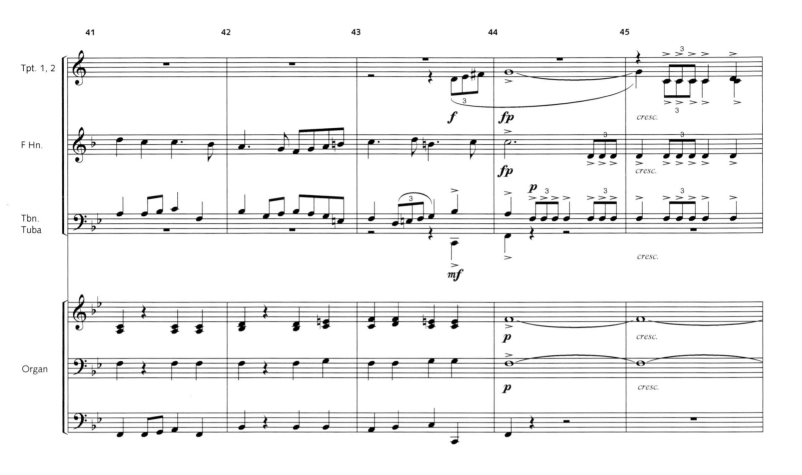

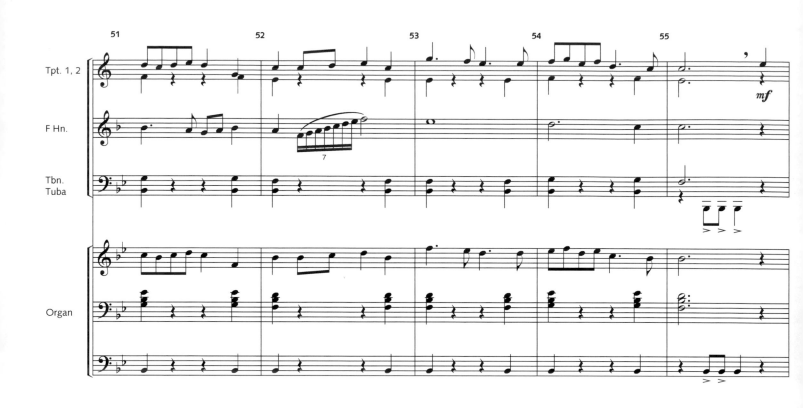

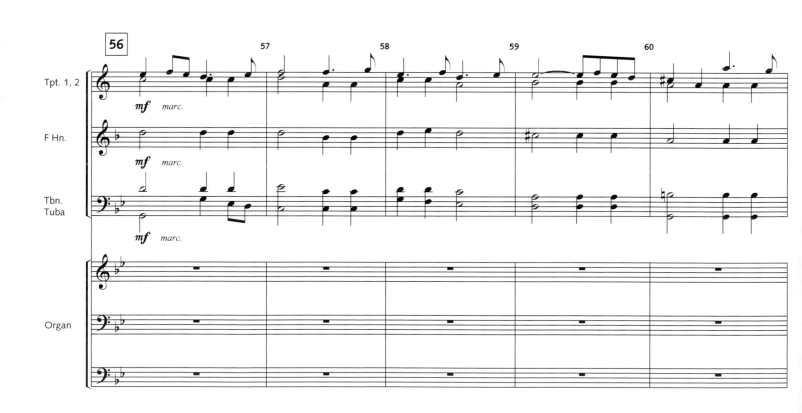

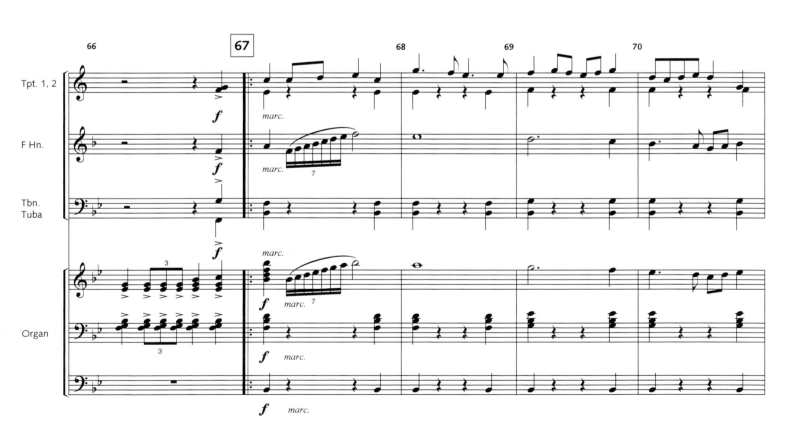

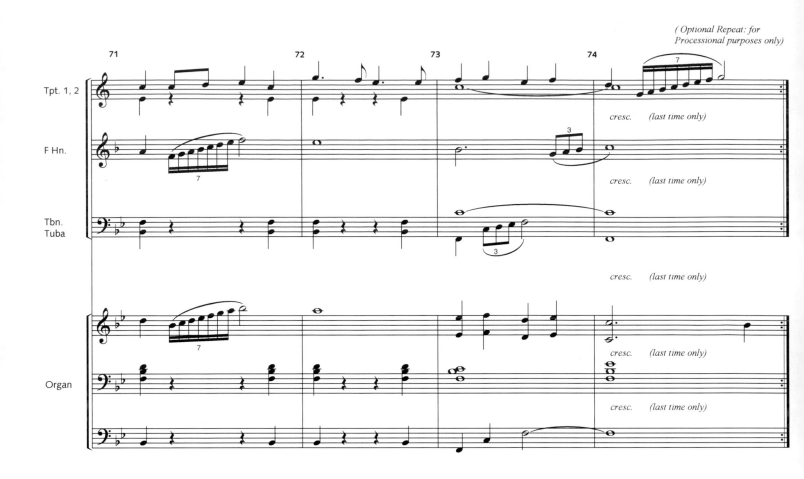

HL44003274